LETTER TRACING FOR KIDS

SAVANNAH

TRACE MY NAME WORKBOOK

Can't Find Your Name?

Have our elves create a personalized book with the name of your choice today!

VISIT US AT:

PERSONALIZETHISBOOK.COM

ABOUT ME

MY NAME IS:

Savannah

I AM [ ] YEARS OLD.

I LIVE IN:

For parents

For kids

DRAW YOU AND YOUR FAMILY

S

Savannah

Savannah

Savannah

Savannah

Savannah

THIS IS HOW I WRITE MY NAME

MY NAME HAS ___ LETTERS

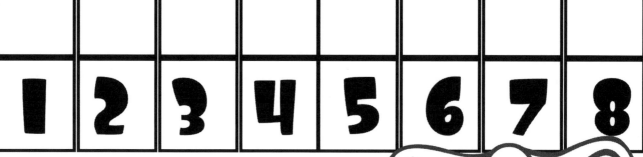

1	2	3	4	5	6	7	8

Savannah

____avannah

_____annah

_____nnah

_____nah

_____ah

COLOR THE EGGS WITH LETTERS OF OUR NAME WRITE YOUR NAME

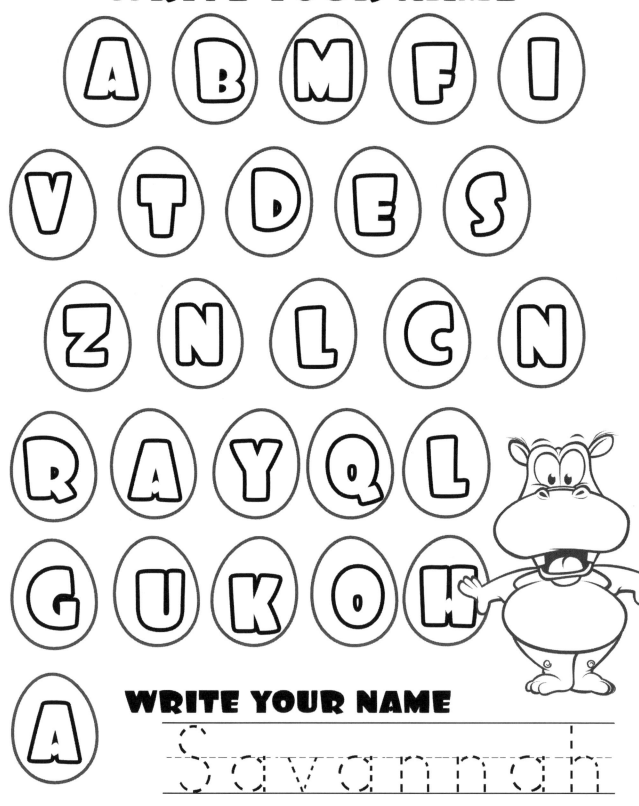

A B M F I
V T D E S
Z N L C N
R A Y Q L
G U K O H
A

WRITE YOUR NAME

Savannah

WRITE YOU NAME WITH.

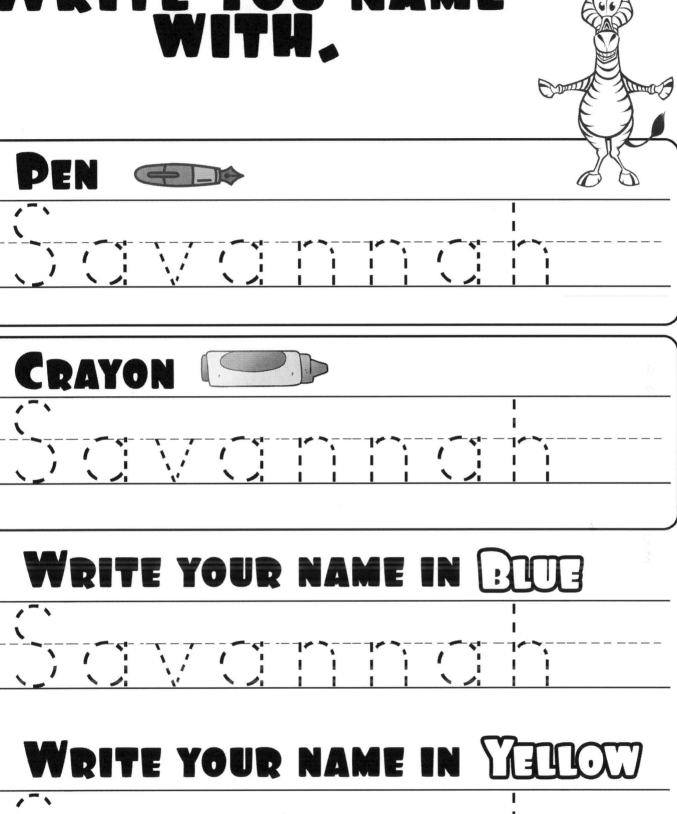

PEN

Savannah

CRAYON

Savannah

WRITE YOUR NAME IN BLUE

Savannah

WRITE YOUR NAME IN YELLOW

Savannah

DRAW YOUR FAVORITE THINGS

COLOR

FOOD

TOY

ANIMAL

MY NAME

My name starts with	My name ends with
_____	_____

FILL THE LETTERS OF YOUR NAME WHITH DIFFERENT COLORS

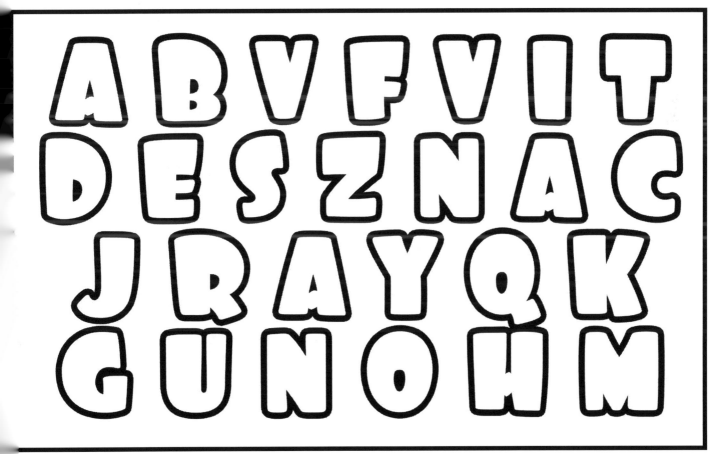

Savannah

Savannah

Savannah

Savannah

Savannah

Savannah

Savannah

Savannah

Savannah

Savannah

Savannah

Savannah

Savannah

Savannah

Savannah

Savannah

Savannah

Savannah

Savannah

Savannah

Savannah

Savannah

Savannah

Savannah

Savannah

Savannah

Savannah

Savannah

Savannah

Savannah

Savannah

Savannah

Savannah

Savannah

Savannah

Savannah

Savannah

Savannah

Savannah

Savannah

Savannah

Savannah

Savannah

Savannah

Savannah

Savannah

Savannah

Savannah

Savannah

Savannah

Savannah

Savannah

Savannah

Savannah

Savannah

Savannah

Savannah

Savannah

Savannah

Savannah

Savannah

Savannah

Savannah

Savannah

Savannah

Savannah

Savannah

Savannah

Savannah

Savannah

Savannah

Savannah

Savannah

Savannah

Savannah

S S S S

S S S S

S S S S

S S S S

S S S S

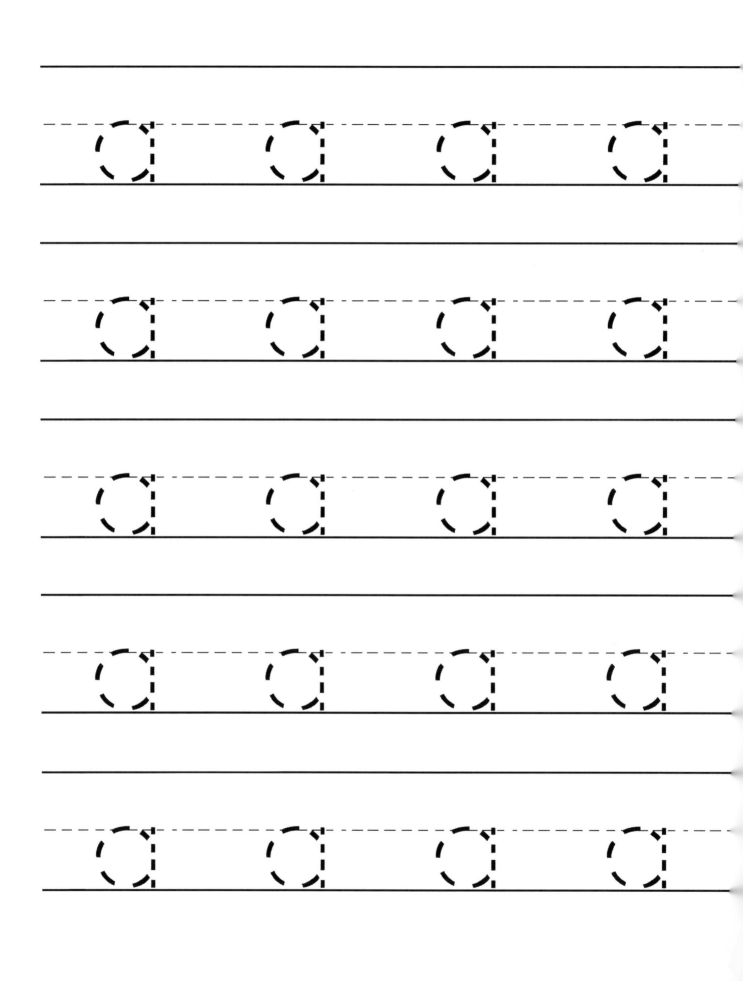

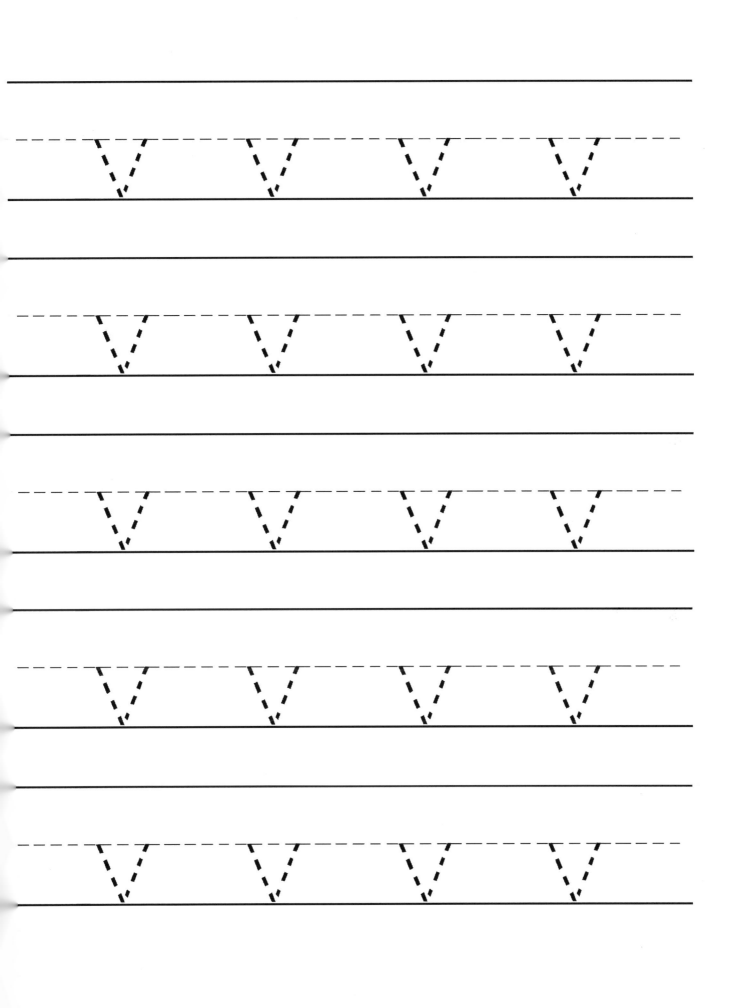

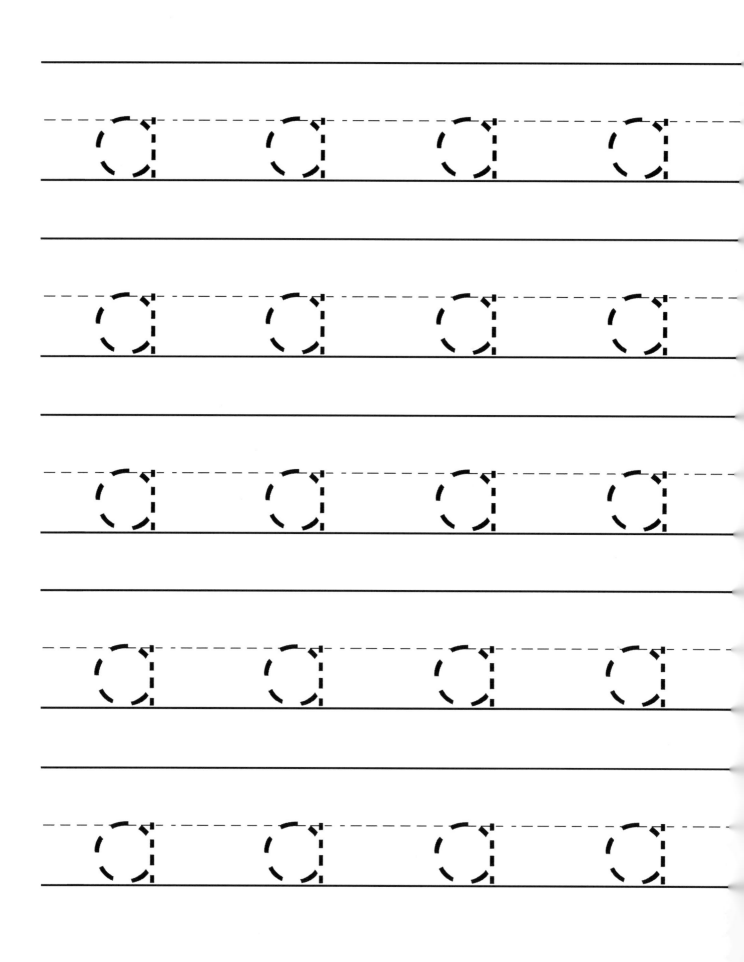

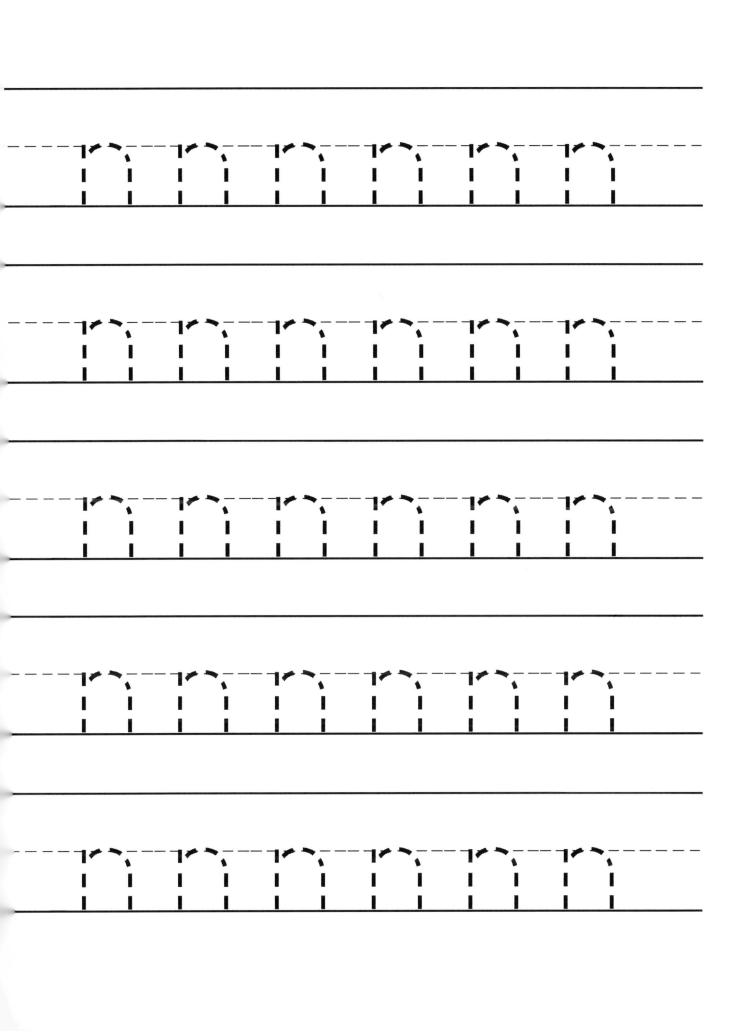

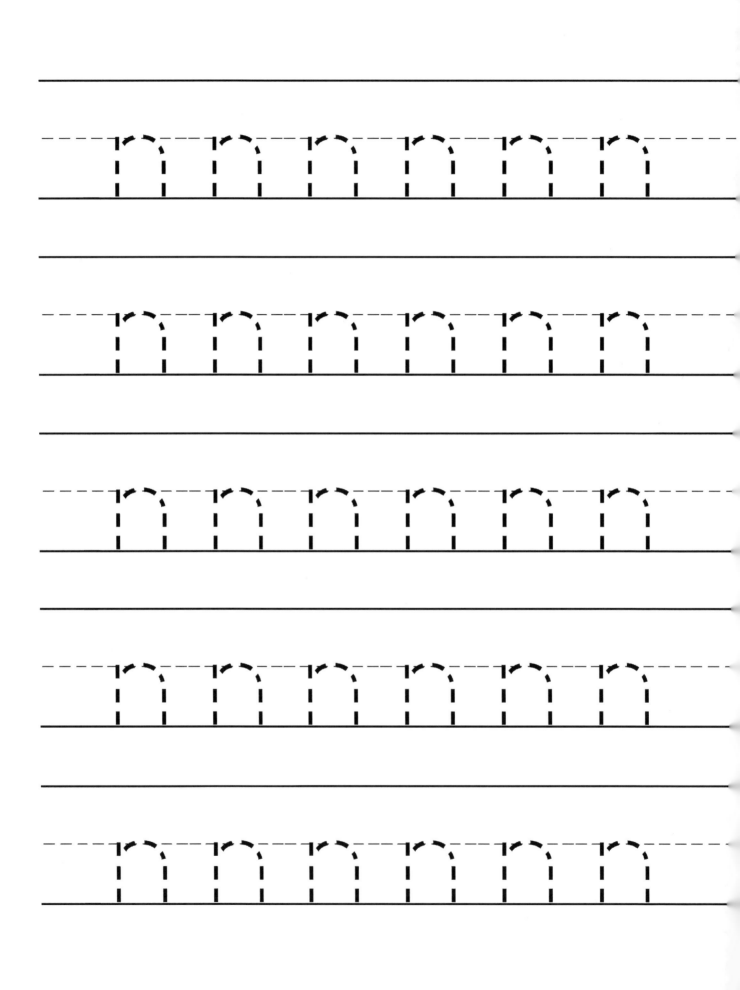

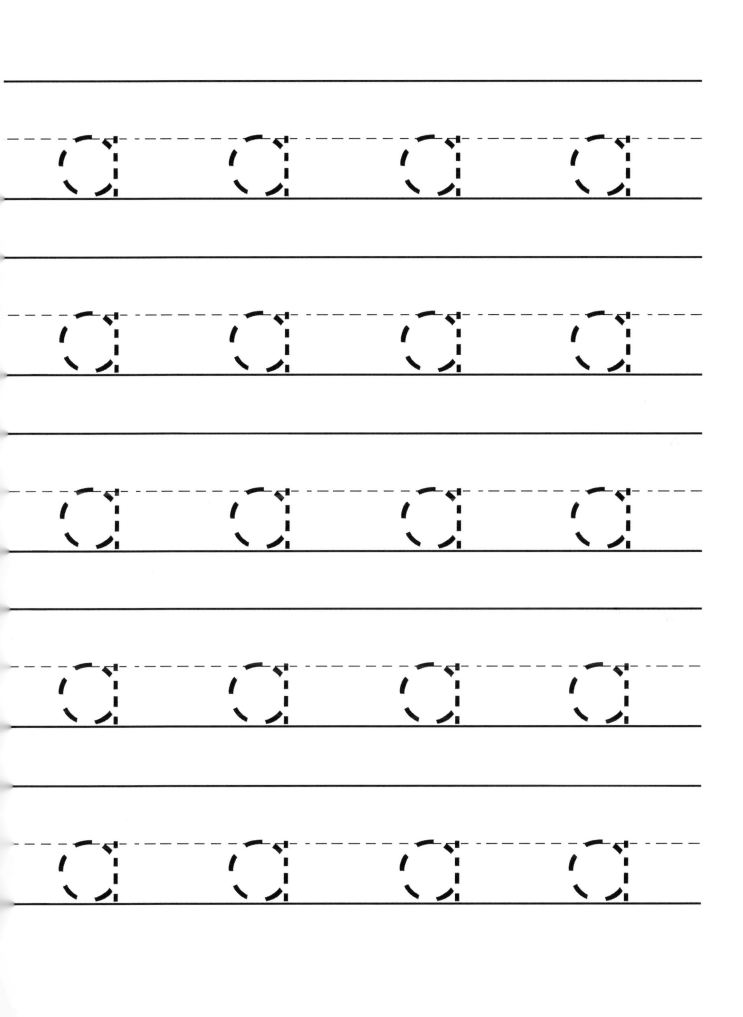

S S S S

S S S S

S S S S

S S S S

S S S S

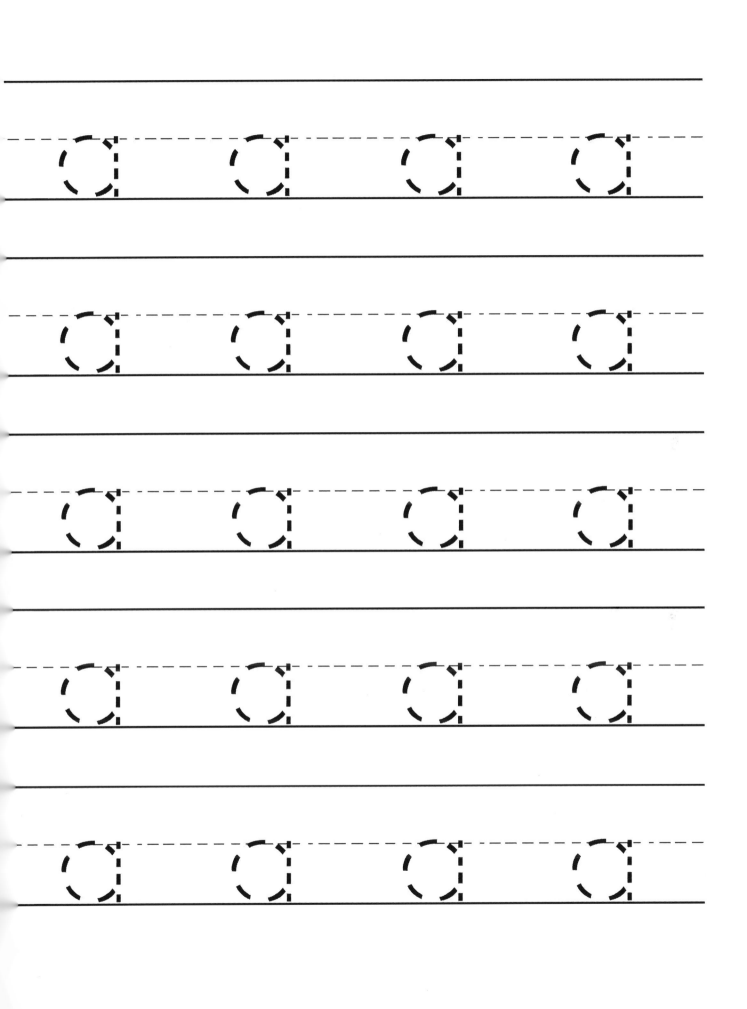

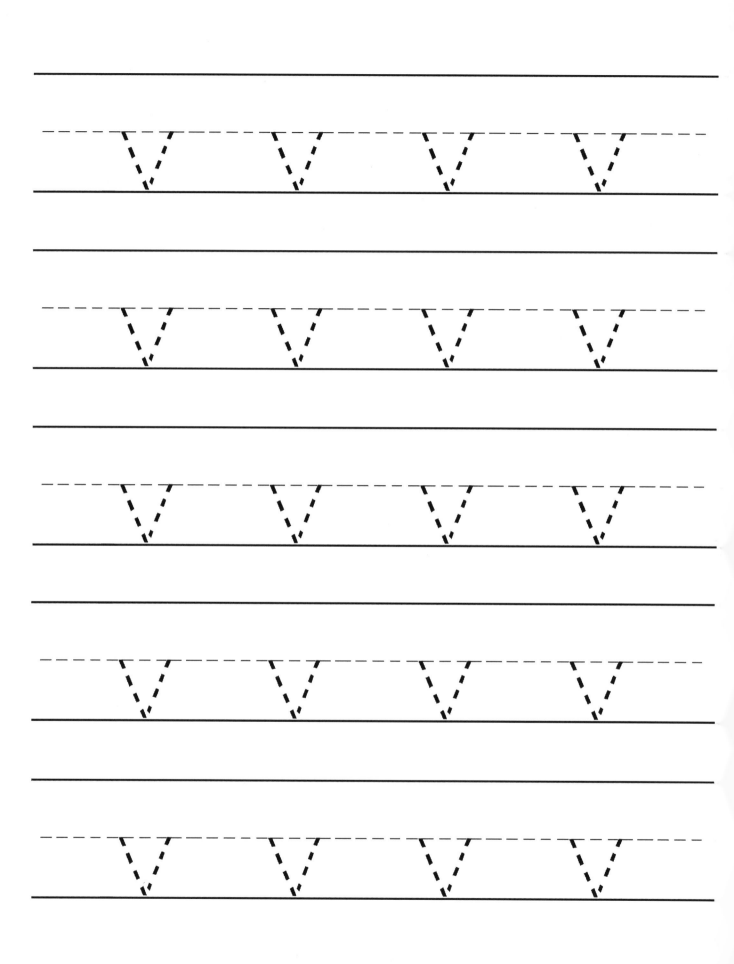

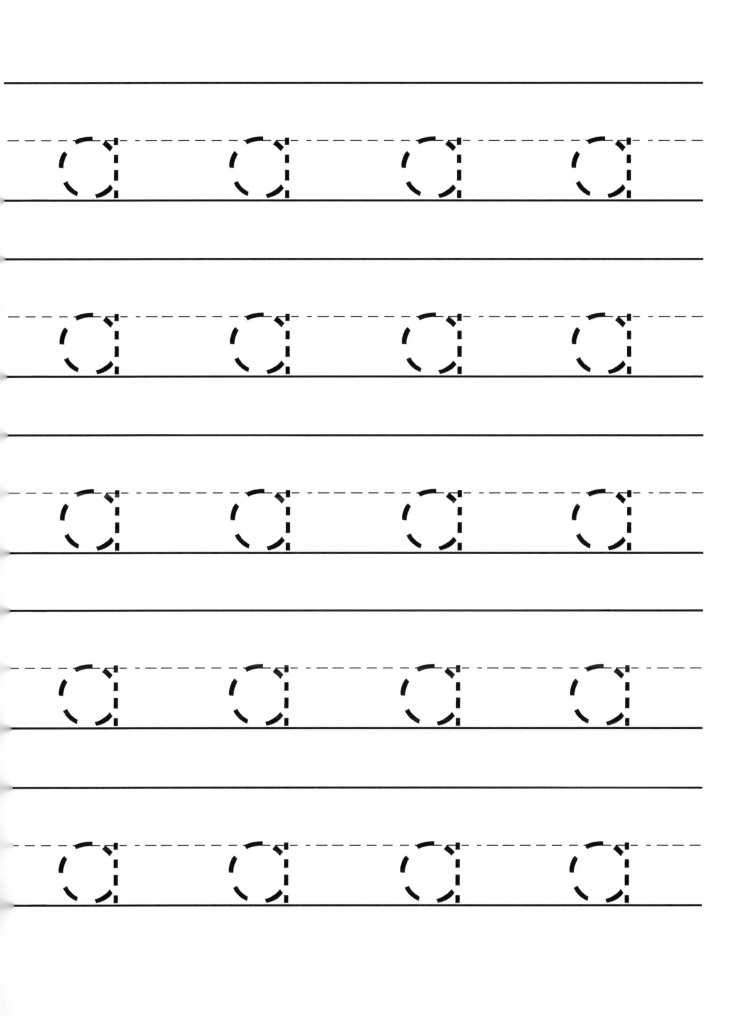

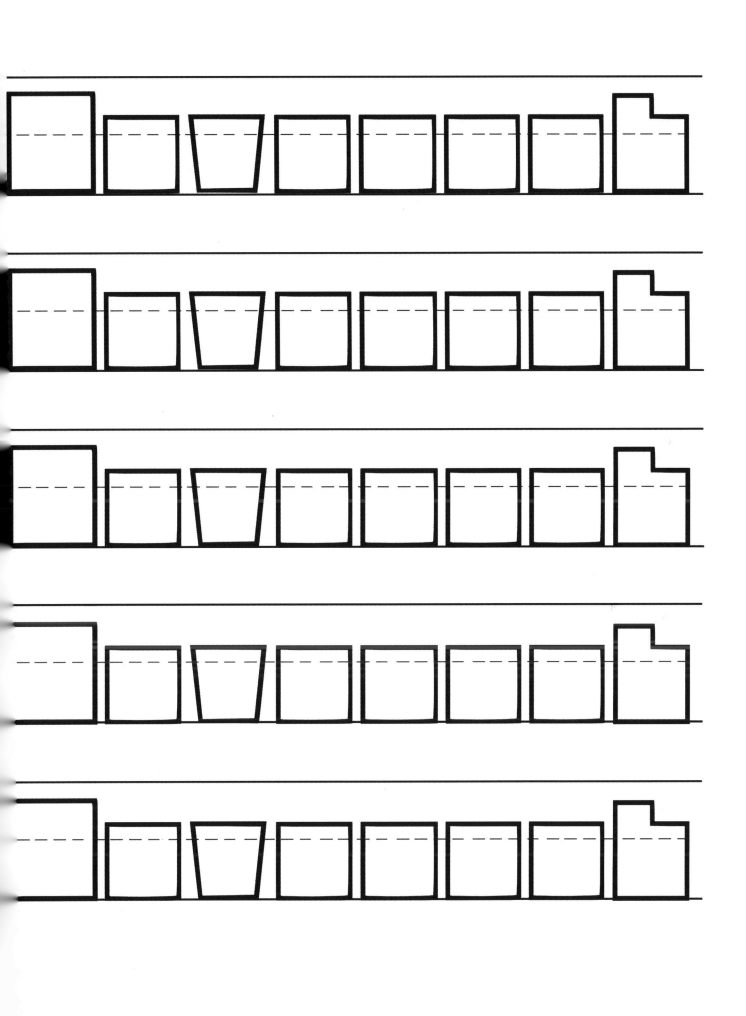

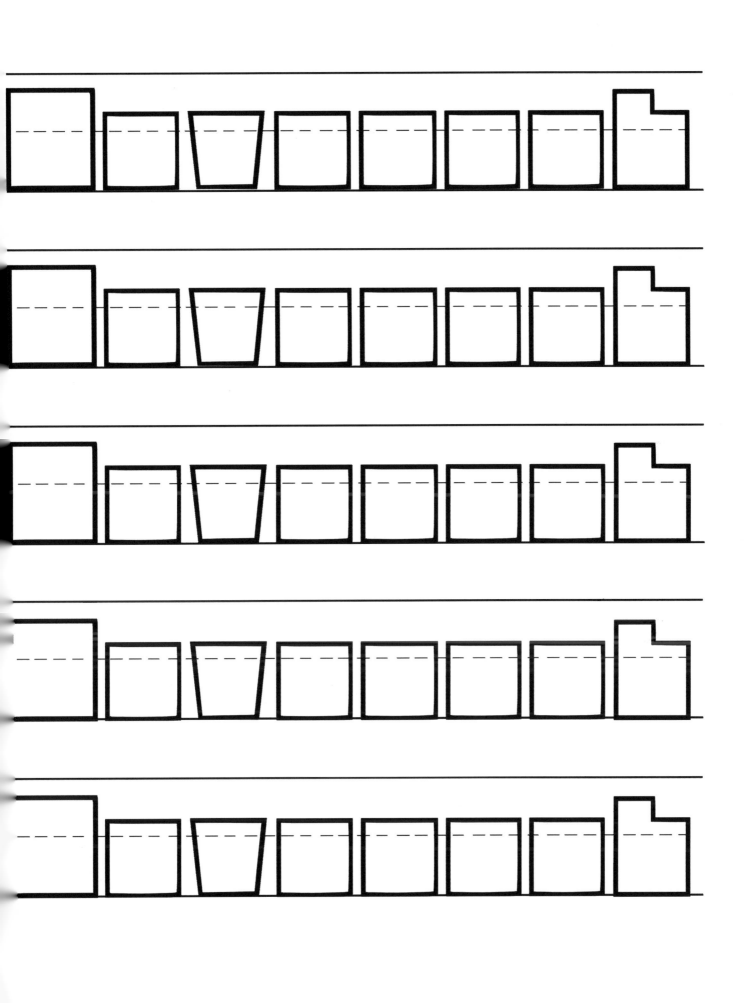

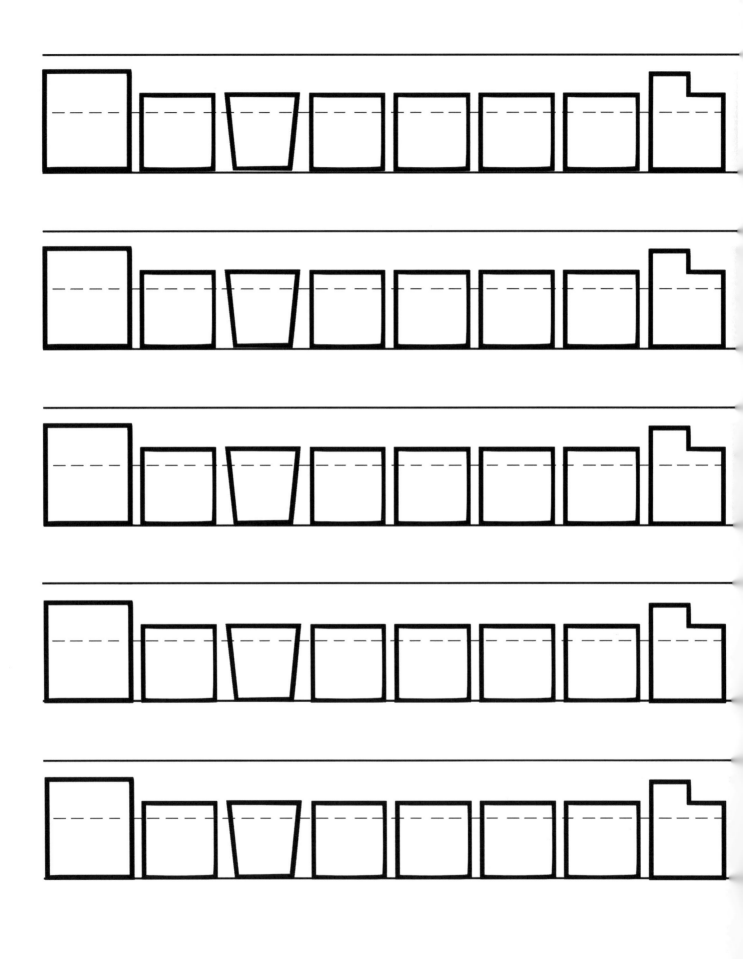

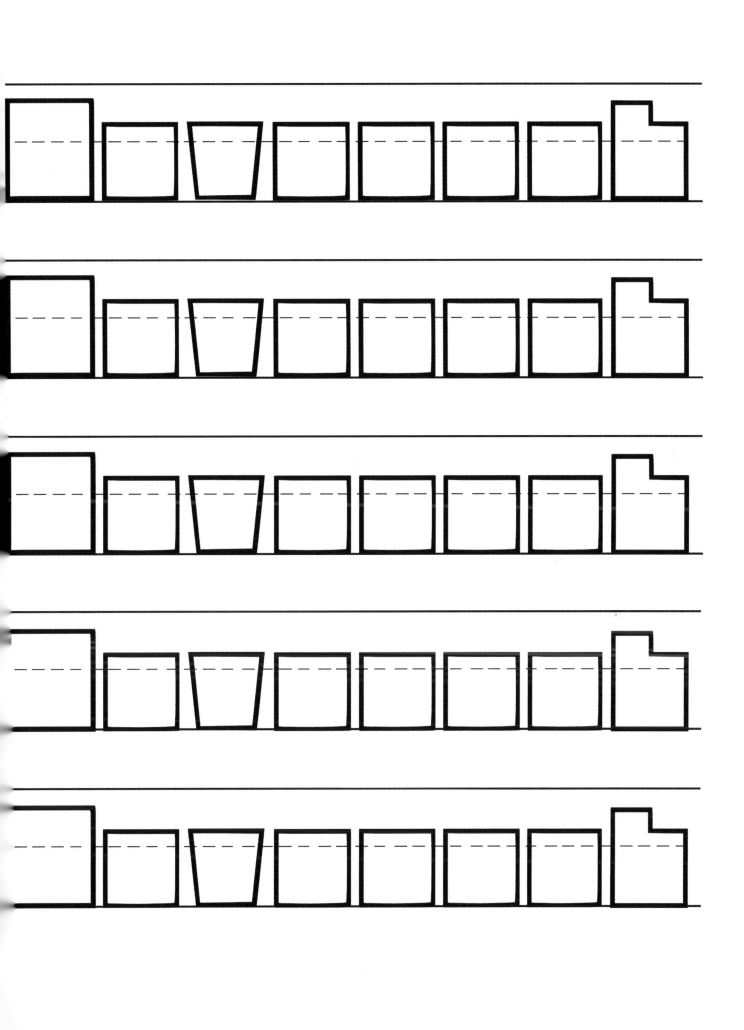

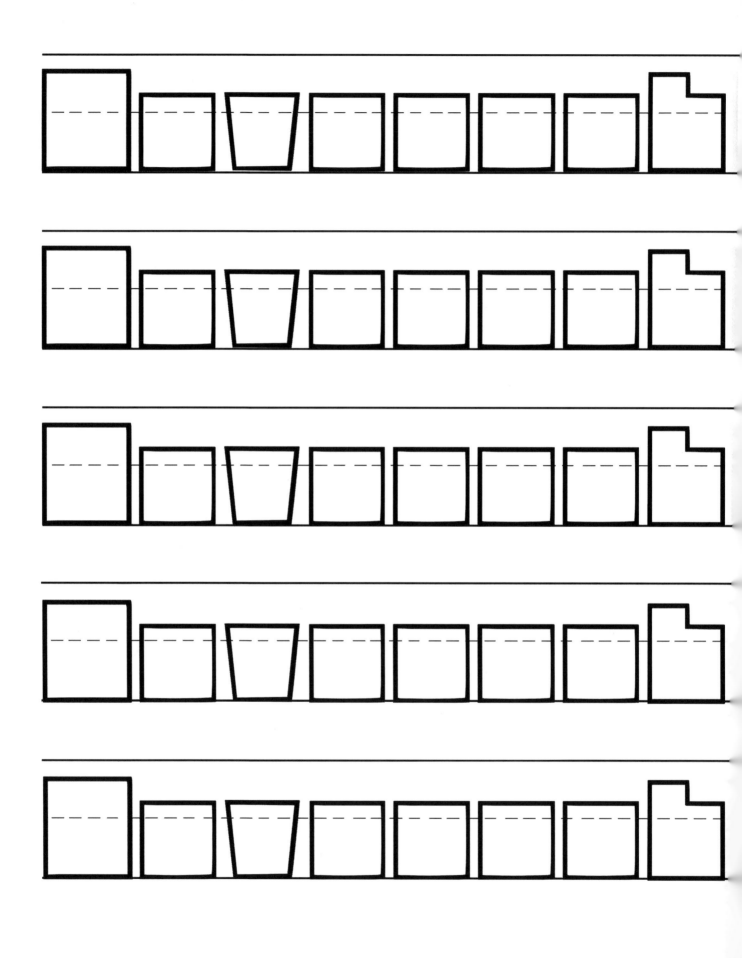

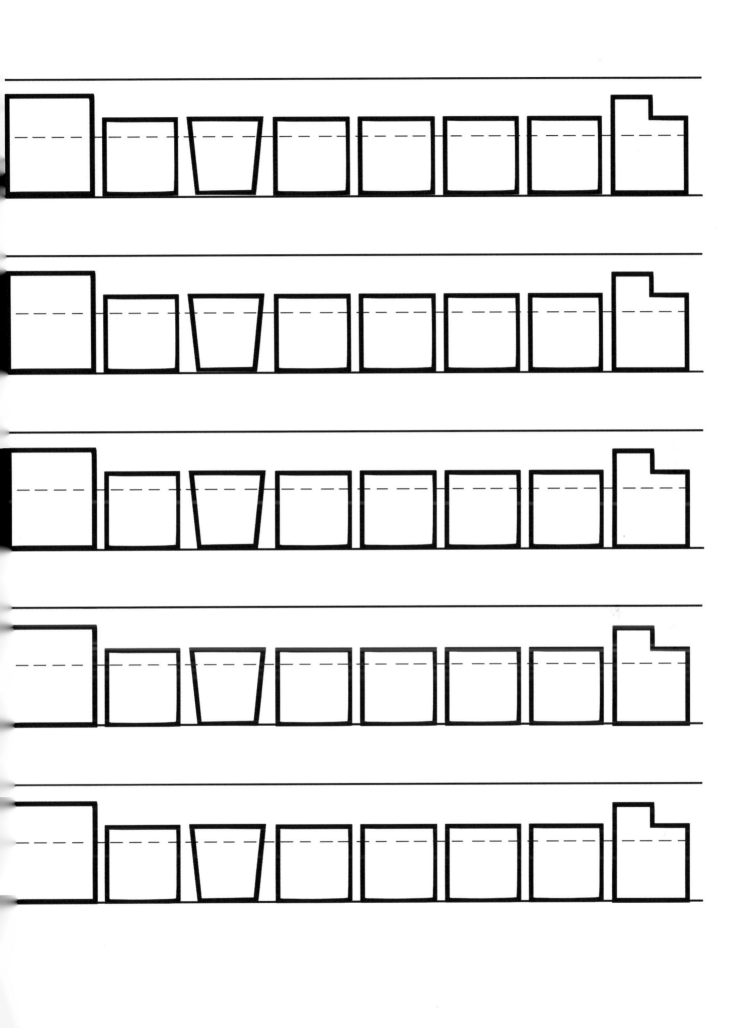

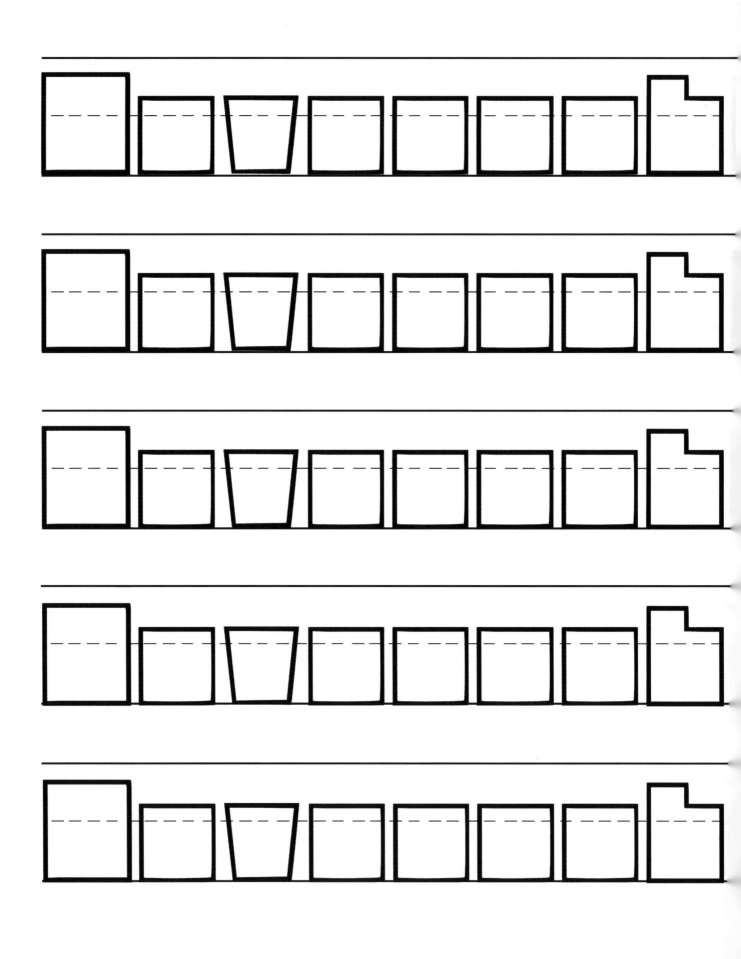

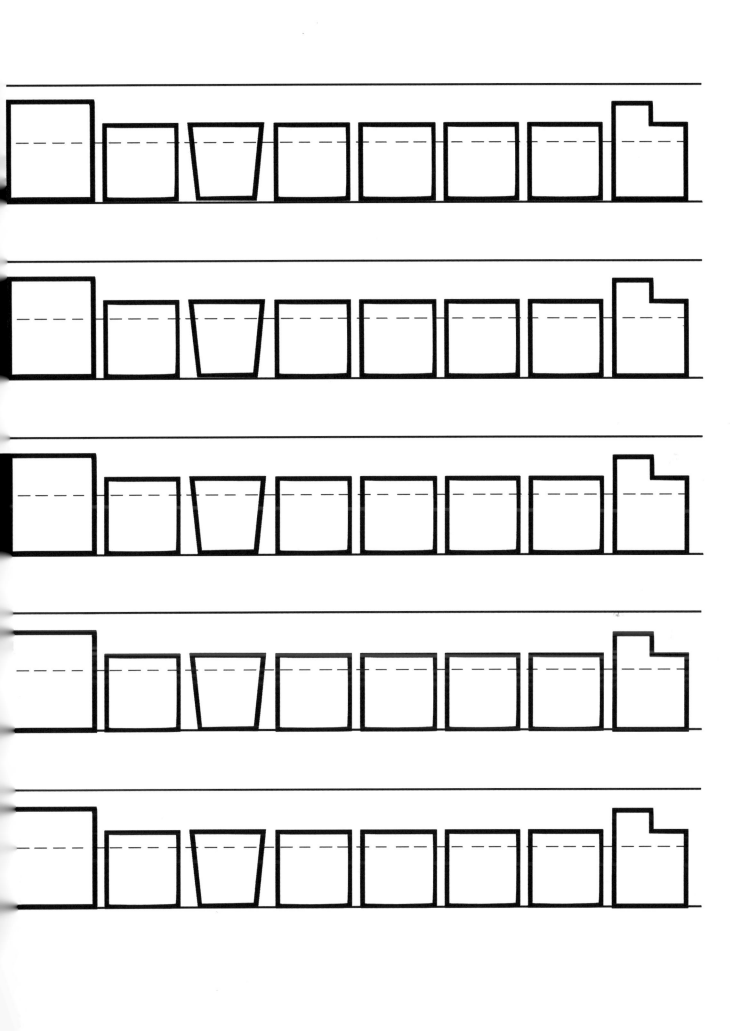

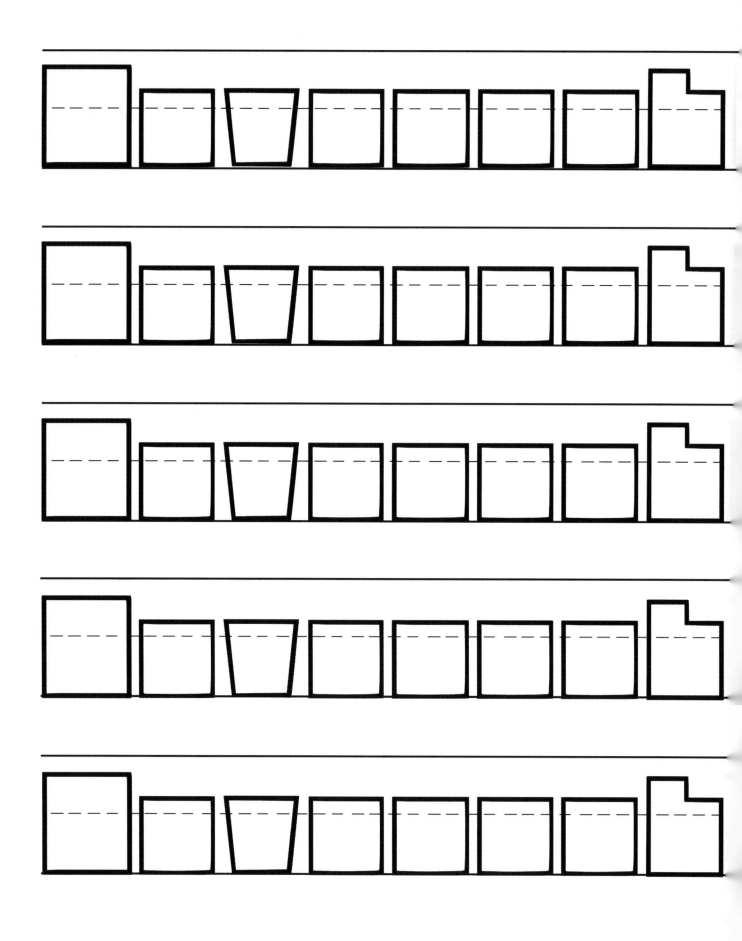

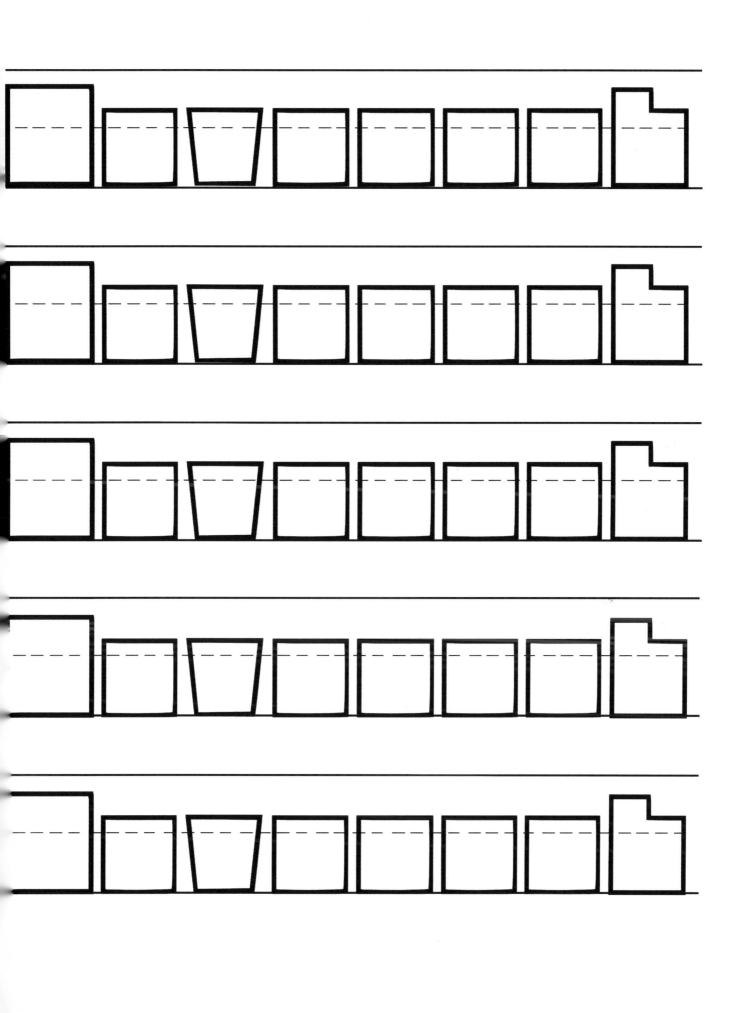

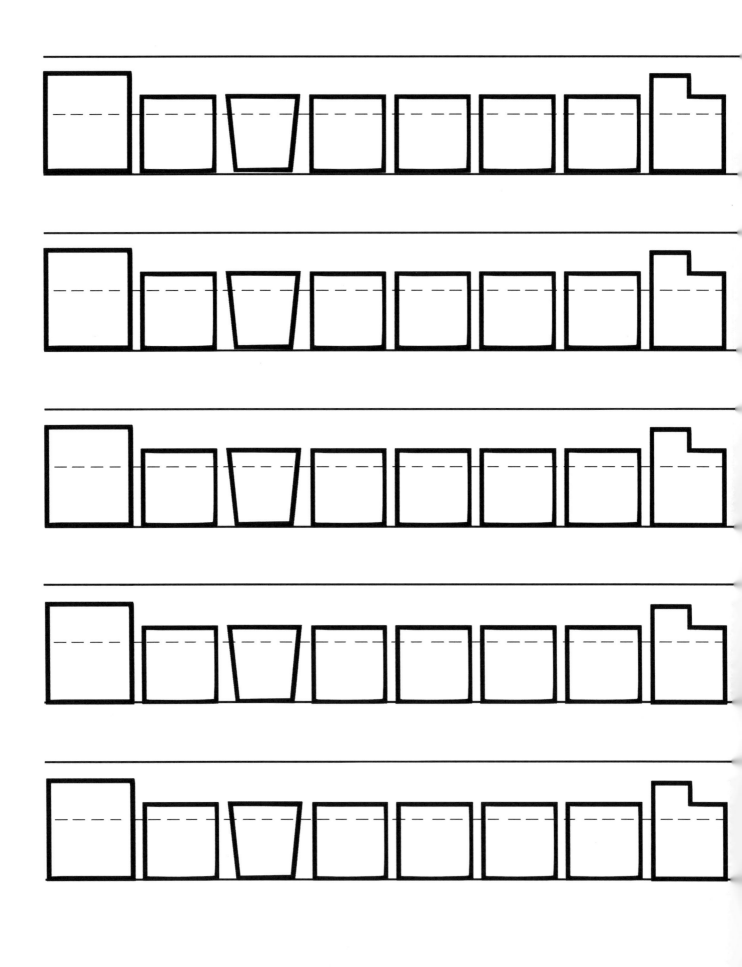

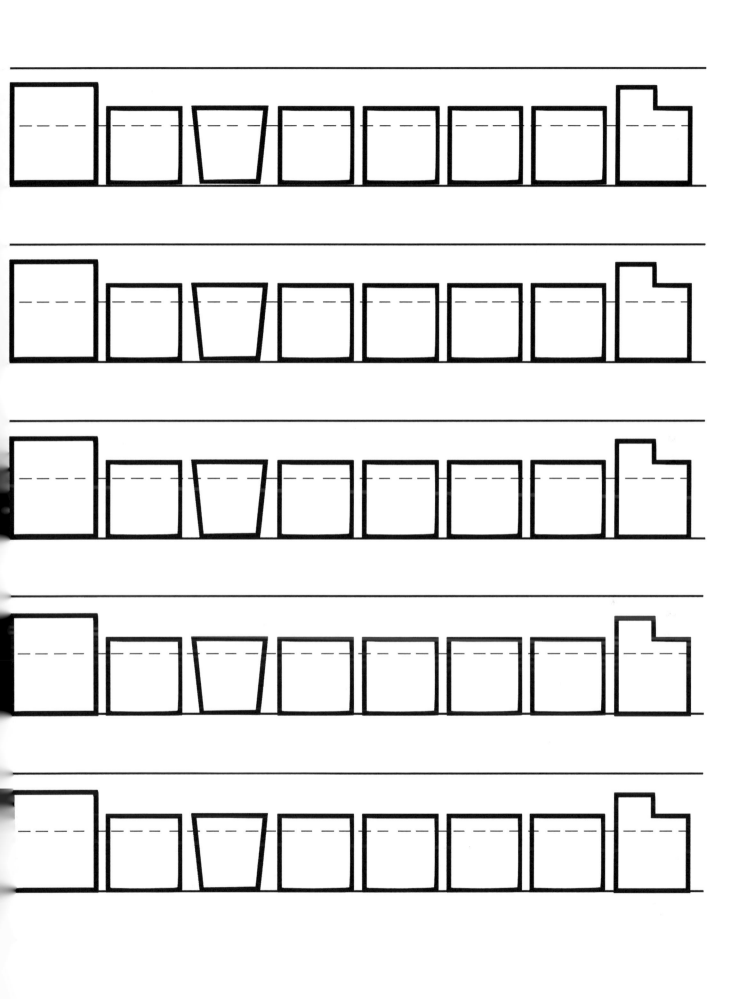

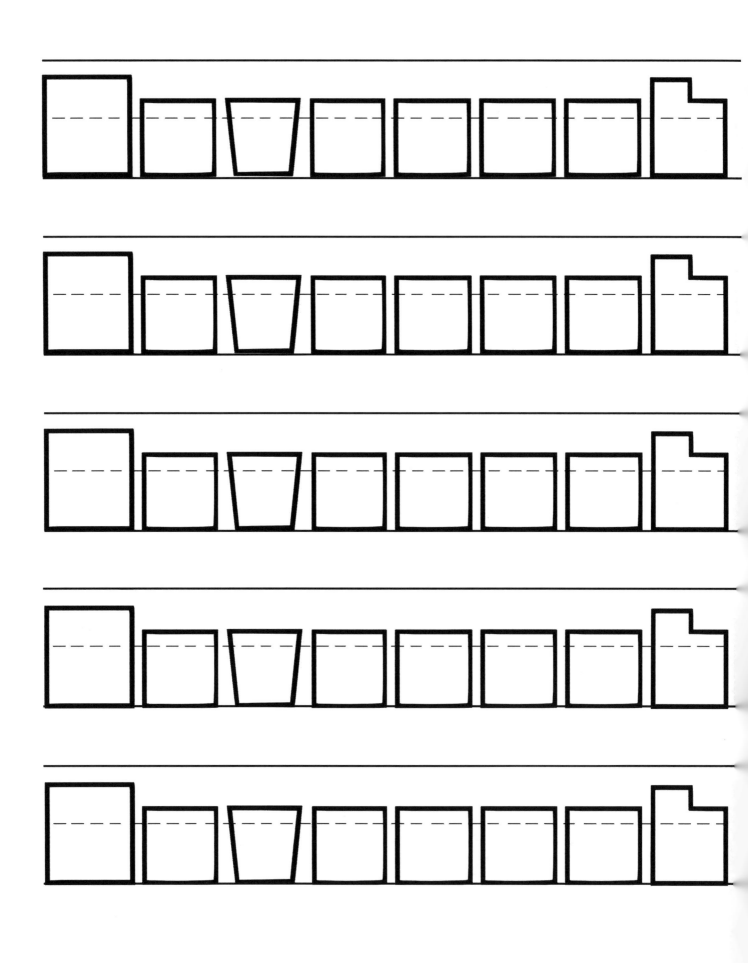

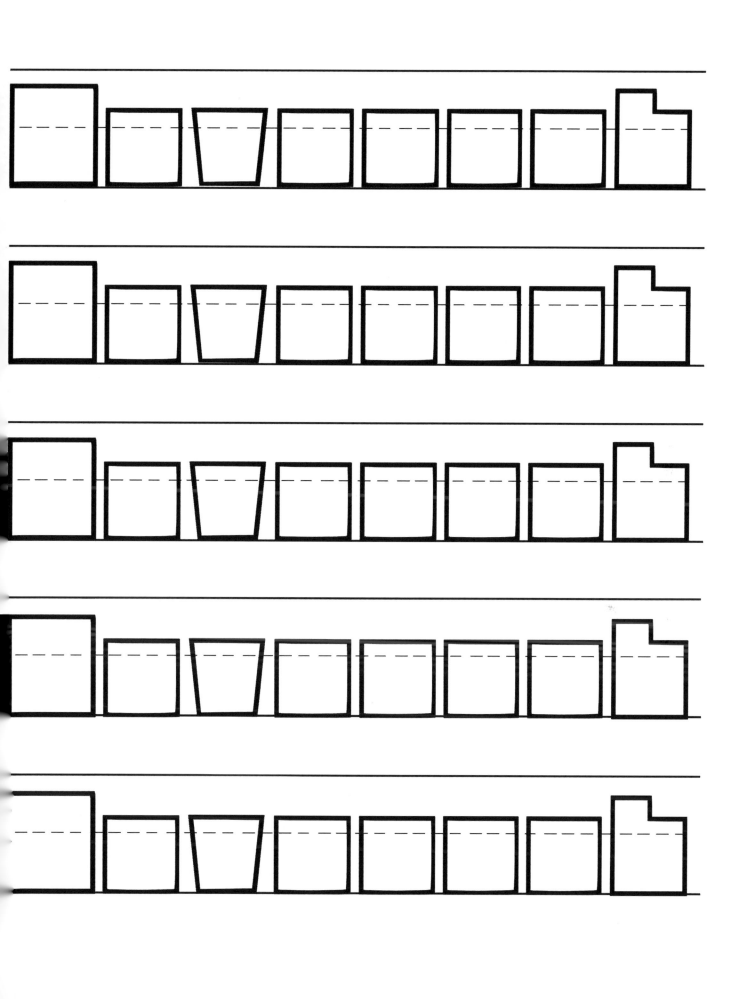

Savannah

Savannah

Savannah

Savannah

Savannah

Savannah

Savannah

Savannah

Savannah

Savannah

Savannah

Savannah

Savannah

Savannah

Savannah

Savannah

Savannah

Savannah

Savannah

Savannah

Savannah

Savannah

Savannah

Savannah

Made in United States
Orlando, FL
08 February 2022

14613288R00057